Life on the Homefront During the Civil War

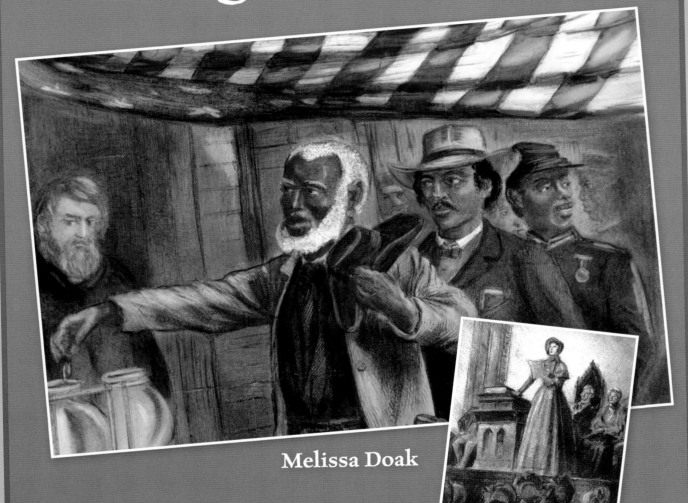

Melissa Doak

CRABTREE
Publishing Company
www.crabtreebooks.com

UNDERSTANDING
THE CIVIL WAR

Author: Melissa Doak
Publishing plan research and development:
    Sean Charlebois, Reagan Miller
    Crabtree Publishing Company
Editors: Mark Cheatham, Kirsten Holm, Lynn Peppas
Proofreader: Wendy Scavuzzo
Editorial director: Kathy Middleton
Production coordinator: Shivi Sharma
Creative director: Arka Roy Chaudhary
Design: Sandy Kent
Cover design: Samara Parent
Photo research: Iti Shrotriya
Maps: Paul Brinkdopke
Production coordinator: Margaret Amy Salter
Prepress technician: Margaret Amy Salter
Print coordinator: Katherine Berti

Written, developed, and produced by Planman Technologies

Photographs and Reproductions
Front cover: Photo © Civil War Archive/The Bridgeman Art Library;
Title Page (p. 1): Bettmann/ CORBIS/Click Photos; Table of Contents
(p. 3): Chapter 1: North Wind / North Wind Picture Archives;
Chapter 2: Library of Congress; Chapter 3: Library of Congress;
Chapter 4: Library of Congress; Chapter 5: Library of Congress;
Chapter 6: Bettmann/CORBIS/Click Photos; Chapter Opener image:
Library of Congress
Alamy: Everett Collection Inc/Alamy- P27, Photos 12 / Alamy- P38
(top); Corbis: Bettmann/CORBIS/Click Photos- P9, P28, P41, P42;
Eon Images: P34; Library of Congress: P4 (top), P4 (bottom), P7, P15,
P19, P20 (top), P21, P22, P23, P25, P26, P30 (top), P30 (bottom), P31,
P32, P33, P36, P37, P38 (bottom), P39, P43, P44; North Wind/ North
Wind Archives: P6, P13 (top), P13 (bottom), P17; Thinkstock:
Photos.com/Thinkstock – P20 (bottom)

Front cover: An illustration shows a home in Fredericksburg, Virginia,
that has been damaged and looted by the Union army.
Back cover (background): A military map of the United States from
1862 showing forts and military posts.
Back cover (logo): A civil war era cannon stands in front of the flag
from Fort Sumter.
Title page (top): This illustration, entitled "The First Vote," shows
African Americans in the South going to the polls for the first time.
Title page (bottom): Elizabeth Cady Stanton was an abolitionist and
an advocate for women's rights. She is shown here at the first women's
rights convention in Seneca Falls, New York, in 1848.

Library and Archives Canada Cataloguing in Publication

Doak, Melissa J.
    Life on the homefront during the Civil War / Melissa Doak.

(Understanding the Civil War)
Includes index.
Issued also in electronic formats.
ISBN 978-0-7787-5344-5 (bound).--ISBN 978-0-7787-5361-2 (pbk.)

    1. United States--History--Civil War, 1861-1865--Social aspects--
Juvenile literature. 2. United States--Social conditions--To 1865--
Juvenile literature. 3. Confederate States of America--Social
conditions--Juvenile literature. I. Title. II. Series: Understanding
the Civil War

E468.9.D63 2011   j973.7'1   C2011-907472-9

Library of Congress Cataloging-in-Publication Data

Doak, Melissa J.
  Life on the homefront during the Civil War / Melissa Doak.
    p. cm. -- (Understanding the Civil War)
  Includes index.
  ISBN 978-0-7787-5344-5 (reinforced library binding : alk. paper) --
ISBN 978-0-7787-5361-2 (pbk. : alk. paper) -- ISBN 978-1-4271-9943-0
(electronic pdf) -- ISBN 978-1-4271-9952-2 (electronic html)
  1. United States--History--Civil War, 1861-1865--Social aspects--Juvenile
literature. 2. Confederate States of America--Social conditions--Juvenile
literature. I. Title. II. Title: Life on the home front during the Civil War.

E468.9.D63 2011
973.7'1--dc23

2011045066

Crabtree Publishing Company
www.crabtreebooks.com   1-800-387-7650

Printed in the U.S.A./012014/SN20131105

Published in Canada
Crabtree Publishing
616 Welland Ave.
St. Catharines, Ontario
L2M 5V6

Published in the United States
Crabtree Publishing
PMB 59051
350 Fifth Avenue, 59th Floor
New York, New York 10118

Published in the United Kingdom
Crabtree Publishing
Maritime House
Basin Road North, Hove
BN41 1WR

Published in Australia
Crabtree Publishing
3 Charles Street
Coburg North
VIC 3058

TABLE *of* CONTENTS

[In Baltimore] . . . we were fired upon from all parts of the street. I heard the bullets whistle about my ears smartly. At last a stone took me in the head and knocked me down. But I got up immediately and discharged my musket at the rebels, and then kept on the march to the depot. I am here in the hospital with the rest of the wounded. My courage is still good . . . .

—a soldier's account of the Pratt Street Riot in Baltimore, Maryland, April 19, 1861

On April 19, 1861, a regiment of Union volunteers from Massachusetts passed through Baltimore, Maryland, to report for duty in Washington, DC. Southern sympathizers attacked them. Civilians and soldiers were killed and wounded in the riot. When the soldiers arrived in Washington, Clara Barton, future founder of the American Red Cross, tended to wounded soldiers in her home.

Life in the North and South

Civil War erupted in April 1861 between the Northern and Southern states of the United States. Eleven Southern states believed they had the right to leave the United States of America and form their own country—the Confederate States of America. Nineteen Northern states, stretching from Maine to Kansas, joined with four border states to prevent the Southern states from leaving the Union. It took four years of bloody conflict and thousands of lives to settle the issue.

One People, United and Divided

In the early 1800s, Americans in the North and South were similar in many ways. Most Americans were descendents of European colonists, except for Native Americans who were here before the colonies were founded and African Americans who were brought here against their will. Most Americans lived in rural areas and worked on small farms. Most were Protestants, and there were some Catholics and Jews. Americans from the North and South believed they were living out the democratic ideals their ancestors fought for in the American Revolution.

As much as they had in common, Americans had begun thinking of themselves as very different long before the Civil War began. They began to see differences between regions of the country. Most of these differences had to do with the different economies in the North and the South.

Most factories and mills in the United States in 1860 were located in the North. These textile machines wove cloth using far fewer people.

The Economy in the North

Between 1800 and 1860, the economy of the North was transformed by new inventions and technologies. Mills and factories began producing goods that had previously come from Europe. Improved roads, canals, railroads, and steamboats made it easier and cheaper to move goods to market. They also helped workers move to cities to work in factories. **Telegraph lines** allowed people to communicate across far distances. New tools for farming, such as the steel plow and mechanical reaper, helped farmers become more productive. They also helped farmers open up new land in the Midwest for farming.

By 1860, more than 22 million people lived in the North, which was two and a half times more than the population of the South. Three out of four Northerners lived in rural areas while one in four lived in cities. All of the nation's largest cities were in the North. More than a million people in the North worked in factories. Many Northerners also worked on farms. Abundant food from farms in the North and Midwest filled markets across the country. This prosperous economy depended on a workforce of people who were paid for their work. The workforce was different in the South.

The Economy in the South

The **cotton gin** transformed the economy of the South in the early 1800s. This invention made it much more profitable to grow cotton.

Cotton was grown on large farms called plantations. Plantations relied on enslaved people to plant, grow, and harvest cotton. Slaves worked in the fields, and they also worked at skilled trades and served as house servants. Plantations were **self-sufficient** meaning that most of the work, such as shoeing horses, smoking meat, and making clothes, was done on the plantation. Plantation owners were the most powerful people in the South. They generally used their money to buy more land and slaves to grow more cotton. They did not put much money into factories, transportation, or even better farming techniques.

Far fewer people lived in the South. The population was little more than nine million people at the beginning of the war. Of those, 60 percent were white and about 40 percent were African American. Only about 10 percent of Southerners lived in cities. So much land was devoted to growing cotton that not many other crops were grown in the South.

Small farmers grew enough food for their families with perhaps a bit left over to sell locally. With little industry in the South, workers did not have access to jobs outside of farming. Local economies stayed small, and cities did not develop as they had in the North.

The economy in the South depended on growing cash crops such as cotton. This picture shows a cotton plantation on the Mississippi River in the early 1800s.

Tensions Leading to War

With such different ways of life, the North and South were suspicious of each other. They each feared that the other side would gain political control. Southerners wanted to protect and expand slavery into new U.S. territories, including Texas, California, and land in what is now the American Southwest. Many Northerners wanted to outlaw slavery in new territories. Several events increased tensions between the two regions.

Congressional Action

The entrance of new territories into the Union threatened to disrupt the balance of power in Congress between free and slave states. This issue was a problem for many years. In 1820, Congress decided in the

Missouri Compromise that Missouri would be admitted as a slave state but that slavery would not be allowed north of a line that today forms the border between Arkansas and Missouri. Thirty years later, the Compromise of 1850 allowed California to be added as a free state and the Utah and New Mexico territories to determine by popular vote whether they would allow slavery.

The Compromise of 1850 also contained a new law that dealt with escaped slaves. Under the Fugitive Slave Act, Southern slaveholders could travel North and have African Americans arrested, claiming they were escaped slaves. This law made it a crime to help escaped slaves, which made Northern whites angry.

In 1854, the Kansas–Nebraska Act allowed the territories of Kansas and Nebraska to enter the Union and decide the question of slavery for themselves. This cancelled the Missouri Compromise of 1820. Northerners feared that all territories could be opened to slavery, regardless of earlier decisions. Many feared that this might result in outbreaks of violence. They were soon proved right.

BLEEDING KANSAS Anti-slavery and pro-slavery forces collided so violently in Kansas, the newspapers called it "Bleeding Kansas." Farmers in western Missouri worried that if Kansas became a free state, enslaved people would cross the border to be free. Many moved to Kansas to vote for slavery. At the same time, people in the East who wanted Kansas to be a free state organized settlers to move there to vote against slavery. When it was time to vote, thousands of pro-slavery whites from Missouri called "Border Ruffians" rode into Kansas just for the election. While there were only about 1,500 registered voters in Kansas, 6,000 votes were cast. Kansas became a slave state. Border Ruffians returned later to elect a pro-slavery legislature and governor.

Abolitionists did not give up in Kansas. They established their own anti-slavery legislature and governor, and wrote their own constitution. A group of Border Ruffians reacted by attacking the anti-slavery town of Lawrence. They burned buildings, ransacked stores, and destroyed newspaper presses. Kansas settler John Brown led an attack on a pro-slavery settlement. Border Ruffians returned to attack free-state settlements. The violence continued for years, during which about 60 people were killed.

🌠 What Do You Know!

BEECHER'S BIBLES
Henry Ward Beecher was a famous New England preacher from a well-known abolitionist family. Harriet Beecher Stowe, author of *Uncle Tom's Cabin*, was his sister. He collected money to buy supplies for men and women moving to Kansas. He purchased about 1,000 Sharps rifles to arm the settlers and had them packed in wooden crates marked "Bibles" to conceal the contents.

A War in Print

Abolitionist newspapers were distributed widely in the North and often banned in the South. Anti-slavery activist William Lloyd Garrison began publishing *The Liberator* in 1831. In 1833, he helped found the American Anti-Slavery Society, which became a powerful force against slavery. Former slave Frederick Douglass published the newspaper *The North Star*, and wrote several autobiographies of his life under slavery. Garrison, Douglass, and many other abolitionists traveled the country giving speeches and lectures.

Harriet Beecher Stowe, a member of a **prominent** Northern family, published a novel in 1852 that upset Northerners and Southerners. *Uncle Tom's Cabin* tells the story of a respected older slave, Uncle Tom, and his life under three owners. The book made the horrors of slavery real to Stowe's readers, and it sold 300,000 copies in its first year. Southerners were outraged, arguing that African Americans were better off as slaves than the free workers in the North. Southern writers responded with their own books showing slavery as a gentle and kind system that took care of people who could not take care of themselves.

> *Talk! talk! talk! That will never free the slaves. What is needed is action—action.*
>
> —John Brown, spring 1859

John Brown

After his experiences in Kansas, John Brown decided that slavery would not be abolished without violent upheaval. In 1859, he led a group of 18 men in an attack on the federal weapons **arsenal** at Harper's Ferry, Virginia. They took hostages and people were killed. The U.S. Marines attacked Brown and his men and captured them. Brown was tried and hanged. Southerners became suspicious that other attacks were planned to free enslaved people. They feared slave uprisings. While many Northerners did not agree with Brown's methods, they were beginning to believe that slavery must be ended. To many abolitionists, Brown was a hero.

John Brown's violent raid on the arsenal at Harper's Ferry frightened many Southerners. Federal troops captured Brown and put him on trial.

9

The Election of Abraham Lincoln

As a candidate for U.S. president, Abraham Lincoln had a reputation for opposing slavery. Southern states threatened to **secede**, or separate from, the United States if Lincoln was elected in 1860. By the time he was inaugurated in March 1861, seven states had seceded and formed the Confederate States of America. Most Americans did not believe that the tensions would result in warfare. On April 12, 1861, Confederate forces attacked Fort Sumter, a federal fort in South Carolina. This was an outright attack on the United States. The Civil War had begun.

The North and South React

When the war began, thousands of Northerners and Southerners rushed to join state regiments to fight. Both sides felt they were fighting for an important cause. Northerners fought to maintain the popular government.

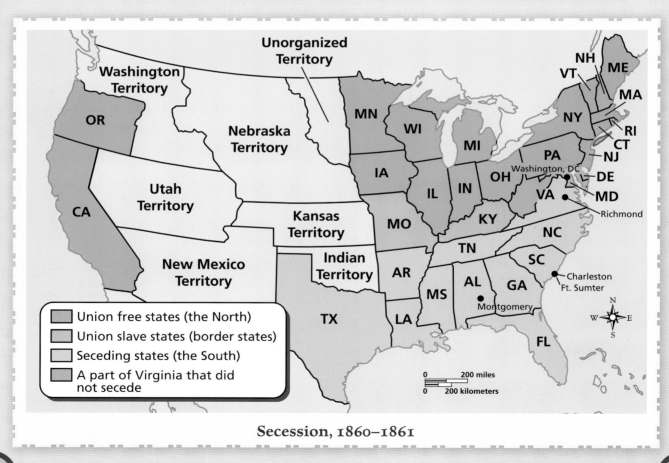

Washington Territory

OR

Unorganized Territory

Nebraska Territory

Utah Territory

CA

New Mexico Territory

Kansas Territory

Indian Territory

MN

WI

IA

IL

MI

IN

OH

MO

KY

TN

AR

MS

AL

GA

TX

LA

NH

VT

ME

MA

NY

RI

CT

PA

NJ

Washington, DC

DE

VA

MD

Richmond

NC

SC

Charleston
Ft. Sumter

Montgomery

FL

N
W   E
S

Union free states (the North)
Union slave states (border states)
Seceding states (the South)
A part of Virginia that did not secede

0   200 miles
0   200 kilometers

Secession, 1860–1861

> *There are only two sides to the question. Every man must be for the United States or against it. There can be no neutrals in this war; only patriots—or traitors.*
>
> —Stephen Douglas, May 1, 1861

Southerners fought to defend the South's way of life and for the right of states to govern themselves. Most people thought the war would be won quickly. Southerners believed Northerners would not fight long to keep the South as part of the Union once they saw how determined the South was to separate. Northerners believed the rebels were too weak and ill-prepared to fight, and they would soon give up and return to the Union.

The Underlying Issue

Neither side admitted that the war was about slavery. The South simply argued it was fighting to preserve its way of life. Northerners also downplayed slavery. They argued that secession was unconstitutional. They fought to keep the North united, since some border states that stayed in the Union, such as Maryland, Kentucky, and Missouri, allowed slavery.

> *Lincoln may bring his 75,000 troops against us. We fight for our homes, our fathers and mothers, our wives, brothers, sisters, sons, and daughters!*
>
> —Confederate Vice President Alexander H. Stephens, April 22, 1861

Effects of the War

The next four years of war would take a toll on the North and the South. Most of the fighting took place in the South. Southerners were faced with the effects of war in a way that most Northerners were not. The Union blocked Southern ports, keeping goods from going in and out. Transportation systems in the South were often disrupted or destroyed by the fighting. That meant food and other essential goods could not be distributed throughout the Confederacy.

The North was less directly affected. Its railroads and canals continued to carry goods to ports, where ships took them to foreign ports. Yet even states that were far away from the battlefield sent thousands of men to serve. By the end of the war, every American was touched in some way.

Economy and Social Systems

The Civil War damaged the economies of both the North and the South. The North, with its stable agriculture and thriving industry, was better able to provide its army with men and supplies. Stuck with an agricultural system that had changed little since the American Revolution, the South found itself unable to respond to the changing needs of a country at war.

The South

The population of the South at the beginning of the war was about nine million people. About three-and-a-half million of these people were enslaved African Americans. Two-thirds of Southern whites, or almost four million people, did not own slaves. These numbers began to change with the outbreak of war. African Americans began to escape to the North. Slaveholders owning more than 20 slaves were **exempt** from the draft, so mostly non-slaveholding white men joined the militia or were drafted. Women took on the work of running farms and supervising slaves. Those at home lived in a world of hardship and **deprivation**.

> *We are without machinery, without means, and threatened by a powerful opposition; but I do not despond, and will not shrink from the task imposed upon me.*
>
> —Confederate President Jefferson Davis, February 1861

Effects of the War on Southern Agriculture

The Southern economy was based on agriculture. More acres were cultivated in the South than in the North. Most of the farms in the South grew **cash crops** such as cotton, sugar, and rice. Cotton was sold to markets in the North or Europe for the production of **textiles**. Southern farmers did not produce the wide variety of food crops produced by Northern farmers.

There were three types of farmers in the South before the war. Wealthy plantation owners, called planters, often owned several farms and used large numbers of slaves to grow cash crops. These farmers were only about one-third of the white population, but they held the most political power as legislators, judges, and other elected officials.

Large commercial farmers used **tenants**, who lived on their land in return for their work, and day workers to grow produce such as corn and wheat and raise livestock. These products were also sold in the North or in Europe.

The largest group of farmers had small plots of land. They produced enough food to feed their families, plus a little bit left over to sell locally. Despite differences in farm size, all farmers were affected by war.

All but a few battles were fought within the borders of the Confederacy. Thousands of farms were destroyed as the North and South battled each other across the South. Both Union and Confederate armies **confiscated** crops to feed their troops.

Southern cotton was sold to textile mills in the North and in Europe.

Effects of the War on Southern Trade

To hurt the Southern economy, the Union decided to cut off the flow of trade to the South. To do this, it set up a **blockade** of important ports. U.S. Navy ships along the east coast and the Gulf of Mexico kept foreign goods from coming in and Southern goods from getting out.

The South responded by buying fast, shallow ships called **blockade runners**. These ships could evade the larger, slower Northern ships and bring badly needed goods and supplies to the South. The blockade was effective enough, however, to hurt the Southern economy.

This Confederate blockade runner (foreground) is avoiding a Union cruiser to smuggle goods to the Confederacy.

Effects of the War on the Southern Economy

Inflation occurs when the cost of goods rises rapidly. Prices for basic necessities and food rose very high in the South during the war. There were two reasons inflation was such a problem. A shortage of food and other goods drove prices up. Too much **currency**, or money, in circulation meant that money could buy less and less.

SHORTAGES The destruction of Southern farms caused severe shortages of food. The blockade made it difficult to import food and goods from other countries. Items that did make it through the blockade were often very expensive. The destruction of Southern railroads by Union forces made it difficult to move food from the country to cities.

Basic necessities became very expensive. A pair of shoes that cost $15–$18 in 1862 rose to as much as $800 in 1864. In 1861, a cord of firewood cost $2.50 but, in 1865, it cost as much as $150.

Farmers and storekeepers were forced to give goods to the government in return for almost worthless Confederate money. In 1863, the government **imposed** a 10 percent income tax. Farmers had to turn over 10 percent of their surplus produce. Southerners had to find ways to survive. People often bartered, or traded, for basic goods such as food. Nevertheless, many people in the Confederacy were seriously malnourished. Many Southerners' lives were shortened by the hunger they experienced during the war.

CURRENCY The Confederate government printed currency to pay for the war. When it could not raise enough money in taxes, it simply

---

What Do You Know!

FOOD SUBSTITUTES
Southerners hard hit by the war learned to make do or do without. The *Confederate Receipt Book*, a cookbook published in 1863, gave the following recipe for coffee: "Take sound ripe acorns, wash them in the shell, dry them, and parch [heat] them until they open, take the shell off, roast with a little bacon fat, and you will have a splendid cup of coffee."

Increases in Food Prices, 1861–1865

	1861	1862	1863	1864	1865
bacon *(per pound)*	12.5¢	75¢	$1.25–$6	$8–$9	$11–$13
beef *(per pound)*		12.5¢	$1–$3.33	$2	$8
butter *(per pound)*	20¢	75¢–$2	$2–$4	$15–$25	$15–$20
coffee *(per pound)*	35¢	$1.50–$4	$5–$30	$12–$60	
cornmeal *(per bushel)*		$3.50	$15–$300	$20–$104	$400
flour *(per barrel)*	$6	$16–$40	$30–$75	$125–$500	$325–$1,000
potatoes *(per barrel)*	75¢		$12–$15	$25	

Source: *Everyday Life During the Civil War* by Michael J. Varhola

printed more money. All paper money included the promise to pay the bearer six months after a peace treaty between the Confederate States and the United States. A Confederate dollar was worth 80 cents in 1861. By 1865, a Confederate dollar had decreased in worth to just one-and-a-half cents. People called Confederate money "shrunken cabbage" because it was almost worthless and could buy very little. After the war was over, Confederate currency was completely worthless.

Confederate soldiers were paid $11 each month, when they were paid. They often sent much of their pay home to their families but, with prices rising almost daily and pay rates staying the same, they were not able to help out much. Many soldiers deserted in response to heartfelt letters pleading for them to come home and take care of their families.

Bread Riots

Starving Southerners were desperate. Bread riots broke out beginning in July 1861, usually led by women. In the spring of 1863, more than a dozen cities and towns experienced bread riots. On April 2, 1863, the most famous riot occurred in Richmond, Virginia. Women organized a mob of about 1,000 people to march to the governor's mansion to protest the lack of food in the city. The mob ransacked about 20 stores, shouting, "Bread! Bread!" Finally, the militia broke up the riot.

What Do You Know!

COUNTERFEIT CONFEDERATE CURRENCY

Northerners printed large amounts of fake Confederate money. This pumped more Confederate banknotes into the South and helped decrease the value of Confederate money. A Richmond, Virginia, resident wrote, "Confederate money is not worth keeping."

SOWING AND REAPING.

[SOUTHERN WOMEN HOUNDING THEIR MEN ON TO REBELLION.

SOUTHERN WOMEN FEELING THE EFFECTS OF REBELLION, AND CREATING BREAD RIOTS.

This Northern cartoon entitled "Sowing and Reaping" ridicules the actions of Southern women. The left frame shows Southern women encouraging men to fight. The right panel shows the women rioting over bread—the result of shortages due to war.

"

About three miles from Sparta we struck the "Burnt Country," as it is well named by the natives, and then I could better understand the wrath and desperation of these poor people. . . The fields were trampled down and the road was lined with carcasses of horses, hogs, and cattle that the invaders, unable either to consume or to carry away with them, had wantonly shot down to starve out the people and prevent them from making their crops.

—Eliza Frances Andrews, The War-Time Journal of a Georgia Girl, 1864–1865

"

The North

At the start of the war, the North had every economic advantage over the South. The Northern economy remained strong throughout the Civil War, despite occasional downturns. In fact, agriculture and manufacturing grew significantly throughout the 1860s, partly in response to the needs of the army during wartime.

The Northern Economy

The U.S. government first tried borrowing money to pay for the war. It issued war **bonds** that it hoped Americans would buy to be redeemed later for the cost of the bond plus interest. However, the bonds did not sell well.

The North then turned to printing paper bank notes called **greenbacks**. Unlike in the South, these bank notes could be redeemed for gold. The North experienced inflation, but it was not as bad as in the South. A one-dollar greenback in the North was worth 39 cents in gold at the end of the war. Greenbacks continued to be used after the war.

Manufacturing in the North

Manufacturing in the North had developed earlier and further than in the South. More than one million people worked in over 100,000 Northern factories. Most of the nation's shipyards and factories that produced weapons were located in the North. Industries that thrived during the war included resources used in the war effort, such as shoe production, iron, firearms, lead, and copper.

The textile industry, for example, suffered at first, as it lost access to cheap cotton from the South. It rallied, however, and turned to production of wool fabric used to produce uniforms for the Union military.

The North had other advantages, as well. Most of the country's coal mines were located in the North. Coal was needed to power factories and steamships. Coal and manufactured goods were transported on canals and railroads. The North controlled almost all of the nation's canals, 70 percent of the railroads, and almost all of its trains and other railway equipment.

Agriculture in the North

Large areas of the North were untouched by the war because most of the fighting was in the South. Since the population of the North was so much larger, a smaller percentage of Northern men joined the army.

Northern agriculture was quite different from Southern agriculture. Northern farms grew many different crops instead of one or two cash crops for export. Northern farmers used new farm tools and techniques such as steel plows, McCormick mechanical reapers, and Smalley's corn plow. The new machines helped farms in the North produce more food than ever before, with fewer workers. Bumper crops in 1861 and 1862 meant there was not only food for those at home and those at war, but enough left over to sell to Europe. Northern farmers made enough money to pay off the money they borrowed to buy land and farm equipment.

Cyrus McCormick's reaper made it easier to harvest grain and used fewer workers.

3 Politics During the Civil War

I n the mid-1800s, disagreements over slavery threatened to divide the Union. As this crisis worsened, people began to think of themselves more as Northerners or Southerners rather than Americans.

Politics Before the War

In the early years of the nation, political parties needed to appeal to as many people as possible. Eventually parties formed that focused on the interests of particular groups or regions. Views on slavery began to divide Americans and their political parties.

The Whigs

The Whig Party formed in 1840. It was against increasing the powers of the president. The Whigs argued that the Constitution had separated government powers into three branches to prevent the president from having too much power. People in the North and the South were members of the Whig Party.

In 1854, Congress passed the Kansas-Nebraska Act. This act allowed people in the two territories to vote on whether slavery would be allowed there. This issue divided the members of the Whig Party. Southern Whigs supported the bill, but Northern Whigs who opposed slavery were angry. The Whig Party split apart.

The Republicans

Northern Whigs worked together with anti-slavery Democrats and some other smaller parties to form a new party that opposed slavery. This became the Republican Party. Republican policies, such as high taxes on foreign goods and improved transportation, appealed to Northern businessmen. Republicans were against slavery in the new territories, but most did not think it was right to ban slavery where it already existed.

Republicans nominated John C. Frémont for president in 1856. He lost the election to Democrat James Buchanan, but he won in 11 Northern states. This showed that the Republican Party was strong. It also proved how divided the country was over slavery. Some Republicans thought slavery was a sin. Others thought it was bad for business because Southern goods made by slaves were cheaper than Northern goods made by paid workers.

In the 1860 presidential election, the Republican Party nominated Abraham Lincoln. Lincoln was a former Whig from Illinois who was against slavery because it betrayed the equality of all men promised in the Declaration of Independence.

This cartoon attacks the Democratic platform during the election of 1856 as being pro-South and pro-slavery. The name Buchanan (the Democratic presidential candidate) appears on the flag. Two slaves are chained to the flagpole. The chained woman asks an overseer, "Is this democracy?" The overseer replies, "We will subdue you."

The Democrats

Most Southern Whigs joined the Democratic Party, the strongest party in the United States at that time. In the 1830s, states eased voting restrictions so more white men could vote. Democrats favored equality—for men like themselves. They believed in limits on government. They thought that Congress did not have the power to end slavery where it already existed in the United States.

Despite its strength, the Democratic Party also divided in 1860 over the issue of slavery in new territories. Southern Democrats wanted to defend slavery there. Northern Democrats wanted to allow people in the

Abraham Lincoln, during the 1860 presidential election

territories to decide for themselves in a vote whether to allow slavery. Southern Democrats became so angry they walked out of the National Convention.

Democrats met again later in the year to choose a candidate for president but, they were still so angry, they met in separate buildings. They also chose different candidates. Southern Democrats chose John C. Breckinridge of Kentucky. Northern Democrats chose Stephen A. Douglas of Illinois.

Democrats were split between their two candidates. Republican candidate Abraham Lincoln won the election simply because the North had more people than the South. Southern states began to secede, or separate from the Union, before Lincoln even took office.

One Nation Becomes Two Countries

> *A house divided against itself cannot stand. I believe this government cannot endure permanently half slave and half free.*
>
> —Abraham Lincoln, June 16, 1858

Southern politicians believed they were acting out the ideals of the American Revolution: freedom, equality, and state **sovereignty**. Sovereignty means freedom from outside control. Southerners did not want to be controlled by the United States, but they did not believe that slavery was the opposite of freedom and equality. When Southern states left the United States, they felt they were repeating what their ancestors had done in rebelling against Great Britain during the American Revolution.

Northern politicians also felt they were upholding the Constitution. The Founders of the United States had fought and died to create the United States of America. Letting the South leave would betray the ideals of the American Revolution.

Jefferson Davis, president of the Confederate States of America

The Confederate States of America

In February 1861, each Southern state that seceded sent delegates to create a new government. Jefferson Davis of Mississippi was chosen as temporary president and Alexander

Stevens of Georgia as his vice-president. They wrote a Confederate constitution, adapted from the U.S. Constitution. They also enacted laws that provided for a wartime army, financed the government by selling **bonds**, and set up a State Department, War Department, Treasury Department, and Post Office. They named Richmond, Virginia, as their capital city.

> *Thank God! We have a country at last, to live for, to pray for, and if need be, to die for!*
>
> —Lucius Quintus Lamar, Mississippi

Resistance to Secession

Not everyone in the South supported leaving the Union. Almost half of Georgia's state legislature voted against seceding. Counties in northwestern Virginia disagreed so strongly with secession that they seceded from Virginia in 1861. Western Virginia rejoined the Union in 1863. Sam Houston, governor of Texas, resigned rather than swear allegiance to the Confederacy. East Tennessee wanted to rejoin the Union but the legislature prevented it from doing so.

Not all Southerners supported secession. This illustration shows a secret meeting of Southern Unionists.

Smaller farmers who did not own slaves were often against secession. Unionists were often threatened with violence from Confederate supporters. While there were anti-war areas in the South, there was no organized political anti-war party that challenged the Confederate government.

Conflict Among Confederates

Disagreements often prevented groups of Confederates from working together effectively. National political parties did not exist during the war, but political groups were formed that often made it difficult to govern.

Some people supported Jefferson Davis's actions and wanted a stronger central government to take control, at least during the war. Some people did not approve of how Davis was running the war and felt that the states should not give up their powers to a central government.

The Confederacy had a weak central government. States often acted independently. For example, Georgia kept men at home to protect the state, rather than send them to serve in the Confederate army.

Ineffective Confederate Congress

The representatives of the 11 states in the Confederate Congress resented the very idea of centralized government. That made it difficult for the Confederate Congress to work together to make laws or agree on policy. The Confederate Congress was often disorganized and chaotic. Disagreements were sometimes even violent. Dissatisfaction could be seen in the high turnover among members of the Confederate Cabinet. During the course of the war, there were three Secretaries of State and six Secretaries of War. Most members of the Confederate Congress disliked President Davis even more than they disliked each other.

> *The state of feeling between the President and the Congress is bad—could not be worse. . . How can God smile upon us while we have such a man lead us?*
>
> —Confederate General Thomas R. R. Cobb, Georgia

Congress did come together occasionally and work with Davis. At the beginning of the war, many soldiers had joined the army for a one-year term. In early 1862, those soldiers were about to be released even though the war was far from over. In April, the Confederate Congress passed three **Conscription Acts**. One extended the length of service from one year to the end of the war. Another act created the first **draft** in American history, requiring men between age 18 and 35 to register for army service.

This Northern cartoon makes fun of the need for the Southern draft. The two men in gentlemen's clothes are being forced into the army. The soldier on the left says, "Come along you rascal and fight for our King Cotton . . ."

SOUTHERN "VOLUNTEERS".

This age limit was increased as the war continued. A third act created an exception for men who owned or supervised 20 or more slaves so they were not drafted. All the laws were unpopular, but the last made people feel that the rich planters who had the most to lose were protected, while common people went to war.

Confederate Elections of 1863

Elections for the Confederate Congress were held in 1863. There were still no political parties. The Confederate government had become increasingly unpopular. Inflation and shortages of food and necessities were getting worse. Bread riots had broken out in a dozen or more Southern towns. Soldiers were deserting the Confederate army and returning home in large numbers to take care of their families.

News from the battlefield was bad as well. The Battle of Gettysburg in June was a devastating defeat for the South. A third of Lee's army, 28,000 men, had been killed or wounded. In July, Vicksburg, Mississippi, fell to Union troops and the North gained control of the Mississippi River from New Orleans to Cairo, Illinois.

The grim news influenced how people voted. When votes were counted, the number of congressmen who opposed the sitting Confederate government had increased from 26 to 41. This number may have been even higher if elections had been held in Union-occupied areas of the South.

THE FOOD QUESTION DOWN SOUTH.

This Northern cartoon focuses on the shortages of necessities in the South. The barefoot Jefferson Davis (left) tells General Beauregard that a pair of beautiful boots has just arrived from the ladies of Baltimore. Beauregard replies, "When shall we eat them?"

The United States of America

While the Confederate government was focused on the goal of becoming its own nation, the government of the Union had trouble deciding what its goal should be. Some people thought that a short, limited war would bring the South back. Some believed that the Union should abolish slavery. Some thought the South should be allowed to leave the Union, since it would eventually return.

> *I have no purpose, directly or indirectly, to interfere with the institution of slavery in the States where it exists. I believe I have no lawful right to do so, and I have no inclination to do so.*
>
> —President Abraham Lincoln, March 4, 1861

Calming the Border States

Even with the Southern states out of the Union, slavery continued to be a difficult issue. To hold what was left of the Union together, Lincoln had to make compromises. Four states along the border—Delaware, Maryland, Kentucky, and Missouri—were divided on whether to stay with the Union or join the Confederacy. While many people supported the Union, some owned slaves. Lincoln needed to assure them that being part of the Union did not mean giving up their slaves.

MARYLAND Maryland was very important to the Union because it surrounded Washington, DC. If Maryland seceded, Washington would be cut off from the rest of the Union. In the end, all four border states stayed a part of the Union.

WESTERN VIRGINIA The small farmers in Western Virginia were not like the wealthy planters in the East. Few owned slaves and many opposed slavery. After Virginia seceded, Unionists from the western counties met at Wheeling and declared that the Confederate government of Virginia was illegal. Eventually, they voted to separate from Virginia and form a new state. Western Virginia entered the Union on June 20, 1863.

SUPPORT FOR THE CONFEDERACY In all states along the border, there were people who supported the other side. About 30 to 40 percent of soldiers from Maryland, Kentucky, and Missouri fought for the Confederacy.

Uniting the Union

Lincoln won the 1860 election with only 40 percent of the vote because Democrats were split. After the South seceded, there was still political disagreement in the North.

REPUBLICANS Republicans in Congress did not always agree with the Republican president. Many wanted to abolish slavery immediately.

What Do You Know!

The Wheeling convention originally called the new state "Kanawha." At the state's first Constitutional Convention, delegates argued over the state's name. Allegheny, Potomac, Augusta, and New Virginia were all suggested. Eventually, delegates settled on West Virginia.

Others supported ending it gradually. Generally, Republicans continued their support of taxes on foreign goods and free labor that helped businesses.

WAR DEMOCRATS Northern Democrats split into two groups. War Democrats supported going to war with the South to keep the Union together. At the beginning of the war, they often voted with Republicans or chose not to vote. Like most Democrats, however, they did not support freeing enslaved people or allowing African Americans to serve in the army.

COPPERHEADS Some Peace Democrats opposed the war from the beginning. Others began to oppose Lincoln as the war dragged on and its purpose shifted. By 1862, Lincoln and Congress had made freeing the slaves an important goal of the war. Lincoln decided to issue the Emancipation Proclamation in 1862, to free all slaves in Confederate territory. Copperheads were Northern Democrats who sympathized with or actively supported the Confederacy. They did not want the war to destroy the old social order in the South by freeing the slaves.

This pro-Republican cartoon shows three important members of the Copperhead Party as snakes attacking the Union, represented by the woman Columbia holding a sword.

Lincoln tried to silence the anti-war Democrats by suspending the right of **habeas corpus**. Habeas corpus is a constitutional right that protects citizens from being held in jail without a trial. The government began to jail Democrats who spoke out against the war.

A Cooperative Congress

The U.S. Congress was able to pass many pieces of legislation that Southern members of Congress had opposed for years. The Homestead Act of 1862 gave the heads of families 160 acres (65 hectares) of public land in the western territories in exchange for living on it for at least five years. Southern Congressmen had opposed this legislation because they had not wanted territories to be settled by small farmers who did not own slaves.

Other important laws were passed by Congress. A series of acts passed from 1863 through 1866 were designed to aid the building of a **transcontinental railroad**. That made it possible to settle the vast western territories. The Morrill Act of 1862 set aside land that states could sell, then use the money to establish colleges. This bill had been rejected in 1859, but was passed in the Northern Congress of 1862. Many of the land-grant colleges, as they were called, are still educating students today.

Chief Justice Salmon P. Chase gives Abraham Lincoln the oath of office at his second inauguration, March 4, 1865.

Election of 1864

By 1864, it looked as though Lincoln might not win reelection. Northerners were tired of war. Many people planned to vote for the anti-war Democratic candidate, George McClellan, who had been the U.S. Army's general-in-chief. Union victories helped Lincoln's campaign. In September 1864, General William Tecumseh Sherman pushed through the Deep South and into Atlanta. The fall of Atlanta gave Northerners new hope that the Union would win the war. Lincoln was reelected with 55 percent of the popular vote.

By the spring of 1865, Northerners were certain the North would win the war and the Union would be saved. Lincoln's second **inauguration** on March 5, 1865, brought thousands to celebrate in the streets of Washington, to watch the inaugural parade and hear Lincoln's speech. Many African Americans joined the celebrations, and the Forty-Fifth Regiment United States Colored Troops marched in the parade. The war ended the following month.

With malice toward none, with charity for all . . . let us strive on to finish the work we are in, to bind up the nation's wounds, to care for him who shall have borne the battle and for his widow and his orphan, to do all which may achieve and cherish a just and lasting peace among ourselves and with all nations.

—from Abraham Lincoln's second inaugural address, March 4, 1865

Politics at Home

Southerners fought for the honor of the Confederacy, while Northerners fought out of duty to the Union. Yet Washington, DC, and Richmond, Virginia, were distant places for most Union and

Confederate citizens. For many, national politics were less important than local expressions of patriotism and community.

Confederate Celebrations

Early in the war, communities hosted large public celebrations to send off regiments of enlisted men to war. The Confederate government dedicated certain days for fasting and prayer. On those days, Confederate troops and civilians at home **abstained** from eating and prayed for victory.

Early in the war, soldiers' funerals were occasions for elaborate ceremonies in the Confederacy. After the First Battle of Manassas (Bull Run), all businesses closed in the city of Charleston, South Carolina, on the day its soldiers were buried. But as the war dragged on, and more and more soldiers were killed, burials were done quickly after each battle ended.

People in the North

Early in the war, people in the North gave large public send-offs to enlisted soldiers. Sometimes towns would sponsor feasts and parades for regiments passing through on their way to the South.

Northerners paid close attention to the newspapers for news from the battlefield. Victories set off major celebrations, especially as the war neared its end. When Richmond fell on April 4, 1865, a 900-gun salute was fired in Washington, DC. People in Chicago built bonfires and sang in the streets.

Northerners also showed their patriotic spirit by holding large public celebrations on major holidays. July 4 was observed with fireworks, picnics, speeches, and parades. In 1863, Abraham Lincoln issued the first "Proclamation of Thanksgiving." He asked Americans to set apart the last Thursday of November to give thanks and praise to God and pray for healing of the nation's wounds.

> *Men, we have fought through the war together. I have done the best that I could for you.*
>
> —General Robert E. Lee to his men after the surrender of his army at Appomattox Court House, Virginia

SURRENDER OF GEN. LEE!

"The Year of Jubilee has come! Let all the People Rejoice!"

200 GUNS WILL BE FIRED

On the Campus Martius,
AT 3 O'CLOCK TO-DAY, APRIL 10,
To Celebrate the Victories of our Armies.

Every Man, Woman and Child is hereby ordered to be on hand prepared to Sing and Rejoice. The crowd are expected to join in singing Patriotic Songs. **ALL PLACES OF BUSINESS MUST BE CLOSED AT 2 O'CLOCK.** Hurrah for Grant and his noble Army.

By Order of the People.

A poster announcing the surrender of General Lee at Appomattox Court House, Virginia, April 9, 1865

Women in Society

Elizabeth Cady Stanton was an abolitionist and an advocate for women's rights. She is shown here at the first women's rights convention in Seneca Falls, New York, in 1848.

The Civil War required that women step into new roles as husbands, fathers, and brothers joined the fight. Most women found the war brought hardship. Many had to struggle just to survive. Some middle- and upper-class women, especially in the North, found the war gave them new freedoms.

Women's Rights

Women had few legal rights in the North and the South. They were not allowed to vote or hold elected office. Married women did not control their own property or wages. Women did not have the same access to education that men did. Most Americans agreed that women belonged at home.

In 1840, women abolitionists were not allowed to enter the World Anti-Slavery Convention in London. The women were angry and vowed to change such discrimination. In 1848, Elizabeth Cady Stanton and Lucretia Mott held the first women's rights convention in Seneca Falls, New York. The women at the convention wrote a "Declaration of Sentiments and Resolutions" that demanded equal rights for women, including the right to vote.

Women in the North

Family life was changing in the North. Industrialization led to more men working for wages outside of the home. The ideal Northern woman stayed at home to raise her children.

Work had been done within the home for centuries. Farmers and their wives made most things their families needed. Even skilled craftspeople often worked at home. As work moved outside the home into factories and offices, though, the family became less focused on producing goods within the home. Families bought food and other products rather than making them. Fewer women spun yarn or made soap at home. More women bought these products with their husbands' wages.

Some women worked in factories, especially textile mills. Most of these workers were single women helping to support their families or saving money for a **dowry**. Usually, white Northern women stopped working outside of the home when they got married.

> *I long to be a man, but as I can't fight, I will content myself with working for those who can.*
>
> —Louisa May Alcott, April 1861

Women's Volunteer Work

During the war, it became acceptable for women to volunteer because of the idea that women were the guardians of their family's morality. Within two weeks of the firing on Fort Sumter, women in the North and South formed 20,000 local aid societies.

AID SOCIETIES Northern aid societies were much better organized than Southern groups. On April 29, 1861, 3,000 women met in New York City and formed the Women's Central Association for Relief, or the W.C.A.R. More than 7,000 chapters of the new relief organization were formed. Members collected supplies such as bandages and medicines for the battlefield. They sewed and knitted clothing for soldiers. They held fundraisers to send money to hospitals near the battlefields.

NURSING The W.C.A.R. provided other opportunities for women. It established the first training program for women to become nurses. Before the war, all nurses were men. Representatives from the W.C.A.R. even met with President Lincoln. He signed an order that created the U.S. Sanitary Commission out of the W.C.A.R. Men ran the Commission's national office and served in its paid positions. Most of the organization's

People in the War

Mary Ann Bickerdyke

Mary Ann Bickerdyke became a Union nurse early in the Civil War. She was nicknamed "Mother" Bickerdyke by the soldiers because of the tender care she took of wounded servicemen. She devoted herself to the care of enlisted men, saying the officers had enough people to look after them. She had the respect of the Union generals and was given anything she needed. Bickerdyke was the only woman that General Sherman allowed in his advanced base hospitals. Sherman arranged for her to ride at the head of the XVI Corps in the victory parade in Washington, DC, at the end of the war.

> *You believe yourselves very generous and think because you have voted this petty sum [to the Ladies' Aid Society] you are doing all that is required of you. But I have in my hospital a hundred poor soldiers who have done more than any of you. Who of you would contribute a leg, an arm or an eye, instead of what you have done?*
>
> —Mary Ann "Mother" Bickerdyke, address to the Milwaukee Chamber of Commerce

tens of thousands of volunteers, however, were women.

The U.S. Sanitary Commission sent volunteer and paid female nurses to army camps and hospitals. The Surgeon General was so impressed by the Sanitary Commission nurses that he issued an order in July 1862 that required at least one-third of army nurses to be women. By the end of the war, more than 3,000 women had served as paid army nurses. Several thousand others had worked as volunteers.

Women Workers

Northern women also entered the paid labor force to replace men who went to war. Before the war, most women wage earners were single. The war brought new opportunities for married women. Women worked in factories making weapons and as seamstresses making supplies for the troops. They also became "government girls," finding government jobs in Washington DC. In all jobs, women were paid less than men. Government jobs paid women half of what men earned for the same job.

Women taught sewing and other skills in the Freedmen's Industrial School in Richmond, Virginia.

The teaching profession had been open to Northern women for some time. In fact, by 1850, three out of every four teachers in Massachusetts were women. The war opened up even more jobs for women in teaching.

Some women traveled to the South to teach freedmen in Union-occupied areas. Their work was part of a larger volunteer effort to provide aid to freed slaves. Many organizations and churches sent clothing, medicine, and money to the occupied South to care for freed men and women. Hundreds of missionaries and teachers traveled south as part of this larger freedmen's aid movement. The U.S. government established the Freedmen's Bureau near the end of the war to take over these efforts.

Women Farmers

Northern women living in rural areas often took on new responsibilities as a result of the Civil War. They managed farms and homesteads when the men in the family went off to war. Some women, especially war widows with no income, struggled to survive. But most Northern women were not personally affected by the devastation of war.

Women in the South

The Civil War caused women in the South more suffering than it did for Northern women. Battles devastated the land. As prices skyrocketed, women struggled to feed and clothe their families.

Hungry Virginians going for rations in 1864

White Women

Southern ideals of womanhood were different for women of different social classes. Many women were left to deal with difficult conditions on their own because so many Southern men served in the military.

WOMEN ON PLANTATIONS White, upper-class women had slaves to do most of the housework. Wealthy women did much less work than any other group of women in Southern society. Enslaved people cooked, cleaned, served as their personal maids, and raised their children. That meant that wealthy women directly managed the slaves in their homes.

Some upper-class Southern women served the South as spies. In 1862, Belle Boyd gave important military information to Stonewall Jackson that helped defeat the Union at the First Battle of Bull Run.

Wealthy Southern women were expected to be attractive and good conversationalists. They had much less education than did women in the North, although most were taught to read and write. Some were taught music, art, and French, as well as needlework. They never worked for wages outside the home. The purpose of upper-class Southern women's education was to help them make a good marriage.

WOMEN ON SMALL FARMS Lower-class white women usually lived on small farms. They were the wives and daughters of **yeoman** farmers. Sometimes these families owned a few slaves, but most did not. These small farms grew just enough food to feed the family, with sometimes a little left over to sell or **barter** in the neighborhood. Women in small farm families cooked, cleaned, kept kitchen gardens, and raised poultry. They raised children and helped in the fields. Their lives were much like the lives of Northern women living on homesteads or small farms.

NEW RESPONSIBILITIES FOR WHITE WOMEN Life was difficult during the Civil War for white women of all economic classes. A **draft** of all white males between the ages of 18 and 35 went into effect in April 1862. The Confederacy became so desperate for soldiers that, in September, the age was raised to 45 and later to 50. A white man was allowed to stay if he owned or worked on a plantation with 20 or more slaves. That exception helped larger farmers and plantation owners. Since most Southerners owned fewer than 20 slaves, though, most women were left on their own to manage as well as they could.

The wives and daughters of yeoman farmers often had large families to support. Traditional women's work, such as raising food and **poultry**, cooking and sewing, became even more important as families tried to get by with less money. Women depended upon their kitchen gardens for food. Before the war,

> "
> *What is all this struggling and fighting for? This ruin and death to thousands of families? What advancement of mankind to compensate for the present horrible calamities?*
>
> —Mrs. Sarah Butler, letter to her husband Union General Benjamin Butler, June 19, 1864
> "

> *Meal was selling today at $16 per bushel. It has been bought up by speculators. Oh, that those hard-hearted creatures could be made to suffer!*
>
> —Judith McGuire

Southern families spent about $6.65 a month on food. By 1864, that food bill was $400 a month, an amount most families could not afford. Women with kitchen gardens could trade extra fresh fruits and vegetables or canned goods for other foods, goods, or needed services. Women with no access to a garden or field were at the mercy of the marketplace.

Southern women living in rural areas often had to take on new responsibilities when their husbands and fathers were gone to war. Southern white women ran plantations and small farms. The wives and daughters of small farmers worked all day to keep the farm going. Then they would work late into the night sewing or knitting to have something to barter for things they could not produce themselves.

African-American Women

Enslaved women worked extremely hard. They performed many tasks usually done by men as well as by women. Some worked as domestic servants in plantation houses. They cooked, cleaned, and raised the slaveholders' children. Other women worked on small farms with just a few other slaves. They might work in both the house and the fields. Many enslaved women worked on plantations doing backbreaking labor in the cotton fields. Any slave could be beaten for small mistakes.

Even though their lives were hard, slave women formed families and raised children. They lived with and loved their

> *Missus, we're even now; you sold all my children; the Lord took all yours; not one left to bury either of us; now I forgive you.*
>
> —an old slave mother to her mistress, after a battle in which the mistress's last son had been killed

🌀 What Do You Know!

FOOD SHORTAGES

Before the war, butter was often imported from the North. During the war, dairy cows were often slaughtered for meat by civilians as well as Confederate and Union soldiers. Milk and butter were often hard to come by. *The Confederate Receipt Book*, a Southern cookbook, gave directions for a substitute for cream: "Beat the white of an egg to a froth, put to it a very small lump of butter, and mix well, then turn the coffee to it gradually, so that it may not curdle."

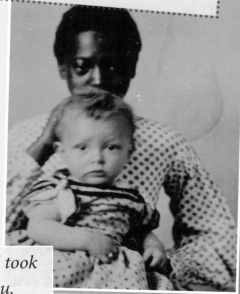

Enslaved women often raised their master's children.

families, knowing that at any time they could be separated by a sale. Slave women sometimes took new husbands when they were separated from their first husband. They also took responsibility for other slaves' children if the parents were sold away from the plantation.

RESISTING SLAVERY Some enslaved women resisted slavery during the war. Black women interrupted work in white households. Sometimes they organized work stoppages in the fields. Others fled with their families behind Union lines.

VOLUNTEER WORK Many free African-American women became involved in aid work to help former slaves. Elizabeth Keckley, a former slave herself, helped found the Contraband Relief Association in Washington, DC, in 1862. This organization raised money to help former slaves. She especially appealed to well-to-do free blacks in the North. She wrote, "If the white people can give festivals to raise funds for the relief of suffering soldiers, why should not the well-to-do colored people go to work to do something for the benefit of the suffering blacks?"

Some black women became teachers for eager black students behind Union lines. Mary Chase, a free black woman, founded the first school for black students in a Union-controlled area in Alexandria, Virginia, in September 1861. Shortly afterward, another free black woman, Mary Peake, founded a school at Fortress Monroe, Virginia.

After the Union allowed African-American men to enlist, free black men and women organized aid societies. As with white societies, they collected money for soldiers and their families, sewed and knitted, provided nurses, and sent food and supplies to African-American regiments.

Most African-American women in the North and the South did all they could to support the Union war effort. After the Emancipation Proclamation took effect on January 1, 1863, they knew a Union victory would mean freedom.

People in the War

Elizabeth Keckley

Elizabeth Keckley's skills as a dressmaker brought her attention from both First Ladies of the Civil War. Born a slave in Virginia in 1818, Keckley was often hired out to make clothing. She bought her freedom in 1855 and moved to Washington, DC, where she opened up her own dressmaking shop. Keckley made dresses for Varina Davis, Jefferson Davis's wife, who offered to take her to Mississippi when the South seceded. Keckley declined and was introduced to Mary Todd Lincoln when Abraham Lincoln became president. Keckley became good friends with Mrs. Lincoln, as well as became her dressmaker. After the war, Keckley published her autobiography, *Behind the Scenes: Or, Thirty Years a Slave, and Four Years in the White House.*

5 African Americans on the Homefront

African Americans led very different lives depending on where they lived in the country. People living in free states had some freedom. They were safe from being separated from their families and loved ones. Enslaved people had no rights. They worked long and hard. They could be punished by whippings or beatings, or sold away from their families. Owners could even kill slaves if they chose.

African Americans in the North

No matter where African Americans, lived they faced discrimination. They were not allowed to vote and they lacked basic rights.

Segregation

Even though they were free, African Americans in the North faced economic hardship and **segregation**. Segregation is when a group of people is isolated from the rest of society. In some states, segregation was not the law but African Americans were still kept separate in schools, housing, and public places. In Philadelphia and in Washington, DC, for example, streetcars had separate areas for white and African-American passengers.

Most African-American children in the North went to public elementary schools. In some areas, they were not allowed to

What Do You Know!

Several Northern states banned African Americans—free or enslaved—from moving there. In 1807, Ohio passed laws to discourage African Americans. In 1844, the Oregon Territory outlawed slavery but also made it illegal for free African Americans to live there. Indiana, Iowa, and Illinois passed laws in the early 1850s that banned African Americans from living in their state.

attend public schools but often went to private charity schools. Boys and girls attended school whenever possible because the African-American community believed education was important.

Military Service

Many African Americans in the North wanted to fight for the Union cause. The navy allowed them to enlist when the war began. The army allowed them to enlist beginning in July 1862. The Union army did not begin recruiting African-American soldiers until after the Emancipation Proclamation in 1863. Black regiments were kept separate from white regiments. White officers often treated African Americans as if they were servants rather than soldiers.

African Americans in the military received less pay than whites. African-American soldiers were paid $10 a month. White soldiers were paid $13 a month. Black troops of the 54th and 55th Massachusetts regiments took a stand against this treatment. They would not take any pay at all until their wages were equal to those of white troops. Protests led to equal pay in 1864.

African-American soldiers faced horrifying dangers on the battlefield. Confederates threatened to kill any African-American soldiers they captured. Captured African Americans were often sold into slavery. Despite the danger, African-American soldiers were often extremely courageous. The 54th Massachusetts distinguished itself in a charge against Fort Wagner in South Carolina. About half the regiment was wounded or killed.

The 54th Massachusetts regiment in the attack on Fort Wagner, Morris Island, South Carolina, 1863

The question that negroes will fight is settled; besides, they make better soldiers in every respect than any troops I have ever had under my command.

—Union General James Blunt, July 25, 1863

By the end of the war, about 180,000 African Americans had served in the Union army. African-American soldiers made up 10 percent of the army and African-American sailors made up 20 percent of the navy by 1865. The Congressional Medal of Honor was awarded to 25 African Americans in recognition of their courageous service during the Civil War.

Abolitionists

Some free African Americans in the North dedicated their lives to eliminating slavery. The best-known abolitionist during the Civil War was Frederick Douglass. Douglass had been born a slave in Maryland in 1817. He escaped when he was 21 years old and eventually bought his freedom. From 1847 to 1863, he published an abolitionist newspaper, *The North Star*. He was a great speaker and used money he earned from his speeches to help escaped slaves reach safety.

Frederick Douglass was a powerful speaker and leader of the abolitionist movement.

Although she was only five feet tall (1.5 m), Harriet Tubman had a big reputation as an African-American abolitionist. She was born into slavery in Maryland in 1822 and named Araminta Ross. As a child, she was hit on the head by an overseer then suffered from bouts of sudden sleep (narcolepsy) for the rest of her life. When she learned that she was going to be sold deeper into the South, she escaped, journeying several hundred miles (km) to freedom. She settled in Philadelphia but was not content with obtaining her freedom. She made numerous trips to the South, guiding other African Americans to the North and freedom. In 1857, she brought her elderly parents to Canada.

African Americans in the South

Most African Americans living in the South during the Civil War were slaves. Three-and-a-half million enslaved people lived in the South at the start of the war. Forty percent of the entire population of Confederate states were African American. About half of all enslaved people lived and worked on large cotton plantations. Others

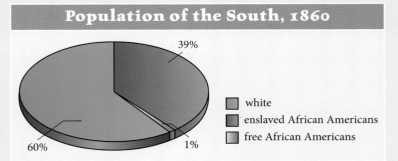

Population of the South, 1860

- 39%
- 60%
- 1%

white
enslaved African Americans
free African Americans

NEGROES FOR SALE.

I will sell by Public Auction, on Tuesday of next Court being the 29th of November, *Eight Valuable Family Servants*, consisting of one Negro Man, a first-rate field hand one No. 1 Boy, 17 years o' age, a trusty house servant one excellent Cook, one House-Maid, and one Seamstress The balance are under 12 years of age. They are sold for no fault, but in consequence of my going to reside North. Also a quantity of Household and Kitchen Furniture, Stable Lot, &c. Terms accommodating, and made known on day of sale.

Jacob August.

P. J. TURNBULL, *Auctioneer*

Warrenton, October 28, 1859.

Printed at the *News* office, Warrenton, North Carolina.

This 1859 announcement for a slave auction explains that the owner must sell his slaves because he is moving North. Some are under 12 years old.

worked as domestic servants, skilled craftsmen, and day laborers. Although they did not have to do the backbreaking labor at cotton plantations, they were still enslaved.

Life Under Slavery

Plantation life was filled with hardships. Enslaved families were crowded into one-room shacks that often lacked heat and running water. They had little clothing and they worked long, hard hours in the cotton fields. If they disobeyed the plantation owner or the overseer, they could be severely punished.

Slaves who lived and worked outside of plantations often had easier lives. Nevertheless, they were still enslaved. Husbands and wives and parents and their children were often separated when they were sold. Children received no education. Teaching slaves to read and write was illegal in all Southern states, except Tennessee.

Slave Resistance

Plantations were often left without overseers and masters during the Civil War. This gave slaves more opportunities to resist their enslavement. Sometimes they refused to work or disrupted work schedules. Sometimes they simply ran away to the safety of the advancing Union troops.

During the war, hundreds of thousands of slaves escaped to the North. Slaves who stayed greeted Union soldiers with joyous celebrations. African Americans sometimes took the opportunity to destroy the property of their masters.

Whites included slaves in their churches, but they preached messages that supported slavery. Slaves sometimes gathered for secret religious meetings. They sang freedom songs and prayed for a Union victory during their secret meetings. African-American lay-preachers inspired their congregation and gave them hope for freedom.

A group of seven contrabands dressed in old Union uniforms at Bermuda Hundred, Virginia

Contrabands

Before slaves were freed by the Emancipation Proclamation, the Union had to decide what to do with slaves in Union-occupied territory.

Many thousands fled their owners to the Union lines. Lincoln and his generals did not want to return the slaves to their owners. Finally, they decided to call these slaves "contraband of war." This meant that the slaves were considered rebel property that was seized by the Union. They were known as contrabands until freed by the Emancipation Proclamation.

Freedman's Village, Arlington, Virginia

Contrabands were still officially property. They lived in camps near Union lines. They sometimes had tents, but they often had very little shelter. Contrabands were put to work in the Union camps or on abandoned plantations nearby. Conditions in these camps could be very rough, but sometimes the Union provided better conditions. A city called Freedman's Village sprang up on the grounds of Robert E. Lee's plantation in Virginia. Freedman's Village had frame houses, a school, a hospital, parks, and workshops to teach trades. It became a model for freedmen's settlements.

Freedom

The Union won the Battle of Antietam in September 1862. After that victory, Lincoln decided to issue the Emancipation Proclamation. He said that he had promised God that if the Confederates were driven out of Maryland, he would free the slaves. Lincoln argued that his war powers allowed him to seize enemy property. He issued the preliminary Emancipation Proclamation on September 22, 1862. It declared that slaves in any states in rebellion on January 1, 1863, would be free. This left slaves enslaved in the border states that were loyal to the Union.

Lincoln Issues the Emancipation Proclamation

Northern Democrats opposed **emancipation** of the slaves. The Democrats gained several seats in Congress when elections were held in November. Some people wondered if Lincoln would still issue the Proclamation on New Year's Day. But Lincoln signed the final Emancipation Proclamation on January 1, 1863, as he had promised.

Celebrations broke out throughout the North and Northern-controlled areas. African-American churches held all-night vigils and rejoiced at the stroke of midnight on January 1, 1863. A crowd of African Americans gathered outside the White House to cheer Lincoln. Those living in Union-occupied territories held huge celebrations. The Union troops occupying the South Carolina Sea Islands held a day of celebration for troops and freed men and women alike. There was a band, a parade, songs and prayers, and a feast. Such celebrations were repeated after Lee's surrender in April 1865.

The Thirteenth Amendment

Republicans in Congress wanted to make sure that slavery would be outlawed forever, everywhere in the country. They wrote the Thirteenth Amendment to the Constitution in 1864. This Amendment abolished slavery everywhere it existed. It easily passed the Senate, but Democrats in the House of Representatives blocked it.

After Lincoln was reelected in November 1864, he wanted to have the Thirteenth Amendment passed right away. The Democratic Party still fought against the amendment, but many Democratic congressmen had lost their reelection bids in November. Lincoln **lobbied** these representatives hard, hoping to get some Democratic support for the amendment. In the vote held in January 1865, 16 Democrats voted for the amendment. African Americans in the gallery cheered and cried when the votes were cast.

Twenty-seven states had to **ratify**, or approve, the amendment for it to become part of the Constitution. By the end of the year, the Thirteenth Amendment became the law of the land. Although Missouri and Maryland had already passed laws to abolish slavery in those states, the border states of Delaware and Kentucky had not. On December 18, 1865, 40,000 slaves in Kentucky and 1,000 slaves in Delaware were freed, ending slavery in the United States.

> *Neither slavery nor involuntary servitude, except as a punishment for crime whereof the party shall have been duly convicted, shall exist within the United States, or any place subject to their jurisdiction.*
>
> —Thirteenth Amendment

✎ What Do You Know!

JUNETEENTH

The news that they were free did not reach most enslaved people in Southern states right away. In fact, those in Texas did not learn that they were free until June 19, 1865, when Union General Gordon Granger arrived with news that the war was over. This was almost two-and-a-half years after the Emancipation Proclamation. African-American Texans began celebrating Juneteenth—short for June 19th—as a holiday with fireworks, barbecues, and gathering together to celebrate freedom. Today, many communities across the United States celebrate Juneteenth.

6 After the War

The United States was not even 100 years old at the end of the Civil War. The young nation was changed forever by a Civil War that split the country into opposing sides. It would take many years to heal the rift and bring them back together.

This illustration, entitled "The First Vote," shows African Americans in the South going to the polls for the first time.

Social Progress

Social changes that resulted from the Civil War led to many gains for African Americans and women. African Americans became full citizens. African-American men gained the right to vote shortly after the war's end when the Fifteenth Amendment was ratified in 1870. Women proved their worth in many different occupations and gained important experience in volunteer associations. These gains would help them in their own struggle for the right to vote.

Much of the old, slaveholding South had been destroyed. The economy of the North, on the other hand, had grown during wartime. The North's prosperity helped the nation thrive for the rest of the century, even though the Southern states were in ruin. The economic inequality between the North and South lasted for many years.

Southern Society

At the end of the Civil War, the culture of the old South had been destroyed. Hundreds of thousands of slaves escaped to the North. Those that remained in the South were freed. Many white Southerners were forced from their homes. The path of destruction left by invading Union troops had devastated the countryside.

Refugees

During the Civil War, about 200,000 white Southerners became **refugees**. Many white Southerners fled their homes because they feared the invading Union troops. Sometimes Union generals ordered Southerners to leave their homes. General William T. Sherman ordered all Southerners to leave Atlanta when he occupied the city in 1864.

Usually refugees were women and children, because most men were at war. Sometimes they fled their homes because of deadly diseases, such as the yellow fever epidemic in Wilmington, North Carolina, in 1862. Many refugees fled to Virginia. The population of Richmond, Virginia, doubled by 1862. People living in areas where refugees settled often resented them for taking some of the scarce food and other aid available.

Refugees faced a difficult life. The government gave some refugees money or other aid. Most refugees had to live in tents, stables, churches, caves, or other temporary shelters. Southern refugees had to decide whether to stay or to flee to the North where there was more hope of finding food and jobs. Most Southerners refused to do so out of loyalty to the Confederacy.

At the end of the war, many refugees returned home. Others had no home to return to. They stayed where they had managed to survive the war, or moved on to other areas, hoping to find work and a better life.

A Civil War refugee family

"
In the name of God and humanity, I protest, believing that you will find that you are expelling from their homes and firesides the wives and children of a brave people.

—Confederate General John B. Hood, letter to Union Major General William Tecumseh Sherman, on Sherman's order for the evacuation of Atlanta, September 9, 1864
"

Ruined buildings in Richmond, Virginia, 1865

Economic Devastation

By the end of the war, the South's economy was in ruins. Farm machinery, railroad tracks, and factories had all been destroyed in the war. Banks had failed and merchants had gone bankrupt. The slave labor system that had supported the economy had been outlawed. Many plantations had been demolished or abandoned. People had lost their homes and faced starvation. Roads and bridges were gone, and many families and communities were isolated. Most African Americans in the South had no homes and no jobs.

At the war's end, the U.S. government faced the task of rebuilding the South. It also had to bring the former Confederate states back into the Union. This process, called Reconstruction, would last from 1865 to 1877.

The North at War's End

While the North had suffered during the Civil War, it escaped the devastation of the South. In fact, the economy of the North at war's end was stronger than it had been four years before. The federal government was much stronger as well.

Before the war, Northerners had invested in technology and transportation. This increased farm and factory production and created new and better ways to take goods to market. New industries, such as steel, emerged. By the late 1800s, manufacturing became more important to the national economy than farming.

The New Nation

The federal government expanded to meet the needs of the nation during wartime. It had gained greater control of the economy. The government now issued paper money and collected an income tax. A new federal bank had been established during the war as well. The government kept its new powers after the war. For the first time, the federal government was stronger than the state governments.

The war had been costly, though. It was the deadliest war in the country's history. Over 600,000 soldiers died—360,000 Union soldiers and 260,000 Confederate soldiers. It would take generations for the scars to heal.

People thought differently about their nation, as well. Especially in the North, people started to think of the United States as one nation instead of a collection of states. They no longer said, "the United States are." They now said, "The United States is."

The African-American Civil War Memorial in Washington, DC, provides tribute to the 209,145 soldiers and sailors who fought for the Union.

> For the present, and so long as there are living witnesses of the great war of sections, there will be people who will not be consoled for the loss of a cause which they believed to be holy. As time passes, people, even of the South, will begin to wonder how it was possible that their ancestors ever fought for or justified institutions which acknowledged the right of property in man.
>
> —Ulysses S. Grant, *Personal Memoirs of U. S. Grant*

GLOSSARY

abolitionist A person who argued for the end of slavery in the United States

abstain To choose not to do something

arsenal A place where military arms and ammunition are stored

barter To trade

blockade Using hostile ships to close off ports and trade

blockade runner Fast, light ship that could slip past the Union blockade to transport goods to and from the Confederate states

bond A certificate issued by the government, in which the government promises to pay the person who purchased the bond the full amount plus interest by a certain date

cash crop A crop that is raised for market and that can be easily sold

confiscated Seized property from its owner

Conscription Acts Laws passed by the Confederacy in April 1862 requiring military service

cotton gin An invention that separates seeds from cotton fibers

currency Money

deprivation People not having what they need

dowry Money or property that a woman brings to her husband when they get married

draft The selection of people for required military service

emancipation Being freed from enslavement

exempt Excused from military service

greenback Term used for U.S. paper money

habeas corpus An order to bring a jailed person before a judge or court to find out if that person should really be in jail

impose To force upon others

inauguration The event and ceremonies that take place when a government official, especially a president or governor, is sworn into office

inflation A continuous, sometimes sharp, increase in the price of goods or services

lobby To attempt to influence a public official, such as a congressman or senator, to support legislation

poultry Birds, such as chickens and turkeys, that are raised for their meat or eggs

prominent A thing that stands out due to its size or uniqueness, or a person who stands out from the crowd as a result of wealth or accomplishments

ratify To approve through the voting process

refugee A person who leaves home to find a safer place to live as a result of war

secede To withdraw from the United States in order to set up a separate nation called the Confederate States of America

Glossary

segregation The separation or isolation of people based on race or culture

self-sufficient Able to take care of oneself without outside help

sovereignty Freedom from outside control

telegraph lines Wires that carry electrical signals that are used to send messages

tenant A person who pays rent to live on or to farm land that is owned by another person

textiles Woven cloth

transcontinental railroad Train system that crossed the United States

yeoman A person who owns and takes care of a small farm

MORE INFORMATION

Books

Clinton, Catherine, editor. *Southern Families at War: Loyalty and Conflict in the Civil War South*. Oxford University Press, 2000.

Faust, Drew Gilpin. *Mothers of Invention: Women of the Slaveholding South in the American Civil War*. University of North Carolina Press, 2004.

Hakim, Joy. *A History of US: War, Terrible War 1860–1865*. Oxford University Press, 1999.

Horn, Geoffrey M. *Sojourner Truth: Speaking Up for Freedom*. Crabtree Publishing Company, 2010.

Massey, Mary Elizabeth. *Women in the Civil War*. University of Nebraska Press, 1994.

McPherson, James M. *The Illustrated Battle Cry of Freedom: The Civil War Era*. Oxford University Press, 2003.

Varhola, Michael J. *Everyday Life During the Civil War*. Writer's Digest Books, 1999.

Volo, Dorothy Denneen and James M. Volo. *Daily Life in Civil War America*. Greenwood Press, 1998.

Wagner, Margaret E., Gary W. Gallagher, and Paul Finkelman, editors. *The Library of Congress Civil War Desk Reference*. Simon & Schuster Paperbacks, 2002.

Ward, Andrew. *The Slaves' War: The Civil War in the Words of Former Slaves*. Houghton Mifflin, 2008.

Ward, Geoffrey C. *The Civil War: An Illustrated History*. Alfred A. Knopf, 1992.

Websites

www.pbs.org/civilwar
The Civil War/PBS. Companion site to Ken Burns's DVD *Civil War*. Includes photos, maps, and video clips.

www.nps.gov/civilwar150/
National Park Service Web Site. In-depth articles, photos, and information on Civil War parks and park events.

www.history.com/topics/american-civil-war
Articles, photos, and profiles of major Civil War figures.

www.civilwar.org/education/students/kidswebsites.html
Civil War Trust Websites for Kids. Has articles, photos, a glossary of Civil War terms, lists of books, and links to other websites.

www.civil-war.net
The Civil War Home Page. Has a photo gallery, lists of books and movies, battle maps, articles, diary excerpts, and reference materials.

www.archives.gov/research/military/civil-war/photos/index.html
The National Archives, Pictures of the Civil War.

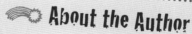 About the Author

Melissa J. Doak, a freelance educational writer, has a Ph.D. in U.S. History and lives in Ithaca, New York.

INDEX